Behaviour Management

Also available from Continuum

Behaviour Management

Tony Swainston

Ideas in Action

network
continuum

Continuum International Publishing Group

The Tower Building
11 York Road
London
SE1 7NX

80 Maiden Lane, Suite 704
New York, NY 10038

www.continuumbooks.com

British Library Cataloguing-in-Publication Data
A catalogue record for this book is available from the British Library.

ISBN: 9781855392311 (paperback)

Library of Congress Cataloging-in-Publication Data
A catalogue record for this book is available from the Library of Congress.

Typeset by
Bookens Ltd, Royston, Herts
Printed and bound in Great Britain by
Antony Rowe Ltd, Chippenham, Wiltshire

Contents

Acknowledgements

Through my twenty years of teaching experience I met many wonderful (and some of them challenging) pupils. I thank each and every one of you for allowing me to develop as a teacher and manager of behaviour. I would also like to thank my wife, a teacher who has taught me so much about the art of communicating effectively with pupils. Finally I would like to thank Dr Tom McIntyre for his support in the writing of this book.

Introduction

Who might use this book?

This book can be used in a practical way, obn a daily basis to remind us all about the key critical aspects of effective behaviour management. It is intended to be used by you as a coaching tool to coach yourself, to coach those adults around you and to coach the students you come into contact with. If you work in a school or college of further education, then it is relevant to you. You might be a headteacher/principal, classroom support assistant, HLTA, bursar or lunchtime supervisor. Whether you are starting out as an ITT student or an NQT or you have 30 years of teaching experience, this book is hopefully relevant. The reason for this is that we are all lifelong learners. In some ways we can also be lifelong un-learners. By this I mean that some of the behaviours we once grew to believe were important can over time be pushed to one side. This is not because we no longer believe in them, but rather that we have forgotten them in the complexity of our own lives and the work we do in schools.

If you work in a school or college, then you will have a responsibility in varying forms and to varying degrees for teaching and learning and the welfare of children. If you feel that you have the confidence to manage, modify and effectively control the behaviour of a class, a group or an individual, then you will also have the confidence to move forward their learning in a way that benefits each individual. This is why effective behaviour management and effective behaviour coaching are so crucial to personalized learning.

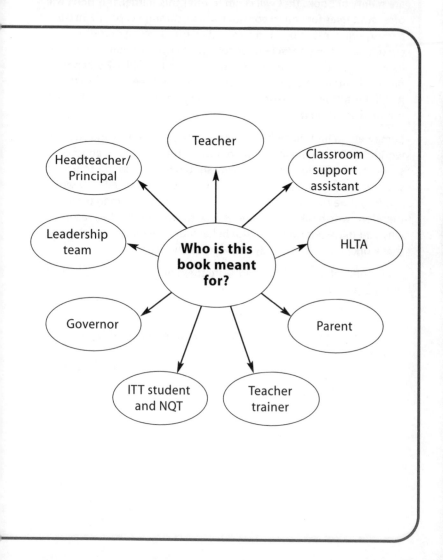

Always adapting to circumstances

This is not a book about the 'rules' of behaviour management. There are plenty of books that will claim to offer this. Rather, this book will offer strategies for you to consider which, through experimentation and experience, can be modified and adapted to match the circumstances in your school or college. If anything that is suggested in the book feels uncomfortable to you, then I would ask you not to dismiss it immediately but maybe try it out and see what you think. If it still doesn't seem to work, then try to discover why this is the case before dismissing it.

Some people find that where certain styles, techniques and strategies worked well for them in one school when they moved to another school they were less effective. Why should this be? In the course of your career, this may well happen to you. Asking yourself now why this might be the case could be very beneficial in the long term. It is, therefore, worth taking a moment now to write down the reasons why you think certain successful behaviour management techniques that work in one school may not work in another.

Try to think of five of these and write them down before you look at the suggestions on the opposite page.

> '*Being ignorant is not so much a shame as being unwilling to learn.*'
>
> Ben Franklin

Can you think of possible reasons why successful behaviour management techniques you have used in one school don't work in another school?

Possible reasons may include:

1   You have built up a reputation in one school where the techniques used are an accepted part of your personal behaviour and style. In a new school it may take a while for you to be known and respected by the pupils.

2   Every school has its own identity and historical journey to its present situation, culture and personality. Behaviours and styles that are successful in one school may simply not be tolerated (at least for the moment) by the pupils and possibly the staff in a new school.

3   Socio-economic circumstances can play a part in how the pupils and possibly the school perceive themselves.

4   Job pressures (for example, you may be multi-tasking more than ever before).

5   Structure pressures (for example, you may be forced to move between lessons more than ever before).

Can you add more to these?

	Further reasons why successful behaviour management techniques used in one school don't work in another school
1	
2	
3	
4	
5	

You should refer back to this if you move school/college or whenever there is change in your work conditions. (So, for example, it is useful to refer back to this list as you move between one year and another or if you get a new headteacher/principal – this can bring about tremendous change for you.)

When we are involved in the education of young people, our primary concern should be to develop their ability to be successful members of the society we call humanity. The five well-known outcomes of the *Every Child Matters* agenda summarize this and can be seen on the opposite page.

What greater job could there be? But this work also carries with it a great responsibility. Schools, colleges and individuals within schools and colleges do make a difference to the life chances of the students that they care for. Another interesting and complementary view of what we should be trying to achieve through education is given by UNESCO's (United Nations Educational, Scientific and Cultural Organization) 'Four Pillars of Learning' – also illustrated on the opposite page. Both the five outcomes of the *Every Child Matters* agenda and the Four Pillars of Learning are useful reminders to us of what we are trying to achieve in our schools and colleges.

Such visions should be central to all that we do. Moving towards becoming more effective behaviour managers and behaviour coaches is easier if we carry with us a key driving force for wanting to contribute to the development and education of young people.

Remember

Let us not leave effective behaviour management to chance. By coaching ourselves, other adults around us and our students, we can move towards a state of order and purpose in all our interactions and endeavours

Advice

Guiding young people through key formative stages of their lives is both an honour and a challenge. As we grow as behaviour managers and behaviour coaches we will be able to have an even greater impact on their progress.

Look at the *Every Child Matters* five outcomes and the UNESCO Four Pillars below. To what extent do you feel you are able to embrace these in the work you do in your school or college?

Every Child Matters – The Five Outcomes

- Be Healthy
- Stay Safe
- Enjoy and Achieve
- Make a Positive Contribution
- Achieve Economic Well-being

UNESCO – Four Pillars of Learning

LEARNING TO BE Developing greater autonomy, judgement and personal responsibility through attention to all aspects of a person's potential	
LEARNING TO LIVE TOGETHER Developing understanding of others and appreciation of independence, to participate and cooperate with others	
LEARNING TO KNOW Acquiring a broad general knowledge, the instruments of understanding and learning to learn	**LEARNING TO DO** The competence to deal with many situations and to act creatively on one's environment

Application

A teacher's motto and the First Golden Triangle of Being an Effective Behaviour Manager

If you had the chance to write a motto for anyone involved in the education and development of young people, what would it include? Pause for one moment and write down your ideas and then look at what is written on the opposite page. Isn't that truly wonderful and isn't it therefore also worthwhile spending some time in getting the basics of effective behaviour management right (and then, hopefully, moving on to being experts!). When we have achieved this, we will have the ability to make an even bigger difference in the lives of children. We can impact on their lives and through this we will influence society both now and in the future.

As an effective manager of behaviour, you will constantly strive for the 'First Golden Triangle of Being an Effective Behaviour Manager'. This includes:

- bringing about order (from regular and unpredictable chaos);
- setting meaningful limits;
- displaying firmness, fairness and kindness.

This kind of outcome doesn't just happen by chance. It needs to be constantly worked at. Once you stop thinking, then young people will step in and invade the vacuum you have left with behaviours that you don't want. Remember you are dealing with experts! The challenge is therefore great, and it may be that you have a series of successes followed by a failure. The importance is to be prepared to keep on learning. Think of behaviour management as a growing, living thing (a plant if you wish) that you need to care for, nourish with new ideas, nurture and prune at times. You should have a plan worked out but one which has the flexibility to be constantly modified through experience, learning and understanding.

Advice

Look at the teachers' motto below. It might be a good idea for you to write your own version of the teachers' motto that you can keep throughout your career.

'A hundred years from now, some things won't matter; how much money was in my bank account, the size of the house in which I lived, or the kind of car I drove around ... but the world may be a better place because I was important in the life of a child.'

The First Golden Triangle of Being an Effective Behaviour Manager

Bringing about order

The First Golden Triangle of Being an Effective Behaviour Manager

Setting meaningful limits

Displaying firmness, fairness and kindness

 Look at the First Golden Triangle (of Effective Behaviour Management). Think about whether these are all part of how you operate on a daily basis.

Application

The Second Golden Triangle of Being a Caring Behaviour Manager

As a caring behaviour manager, you will create an environment where young people are:

- valued as individuals
- respected
- motivated to learn.

This forms the 'Second Golden Triangle of Being a Caring Behaviour Manager'. There is much evidence to support the way that this enables us as adults to build strong relationships with pupils. The Hay McBer Report in 2000 looked at teacher effectiveness and has at the front of it the following words of Year 8 pupils:

A good teacher…

is kind	*is generous*
listens to you	*encourages you*
has faith in you	*keeps confidences*
likes teaching children	*likes teaching their subject*
takes time to explain things	*helps you when you're stuck*
tells you how you are doing	*allows you to have your say*
doesn't give up on you	*cares for your opinion*
makes you feel clever	*treats people equally*
stands up for you	*makes allowances*
tells the truth	*is forgiving.*

If pupils already view you this way you are well on the way to becoming a very effective practitioner and coach of behaviour management. Indeed, for 'good teacher' I think that we can replace this with 'good characteristics of anyone who works with young people'. In fact aren't these the qualities that we would all like to have as human beings?

Advice

Look at the Second Golden Triangle of being a Caring Behaviour Management, below. Think about whether it depicts how you operate on a daily basis.

The Second Golden Triangle of Being a Caring Behaviour Manager

Motivating individuals to learn

Respecting each individual

The Second Golden Triangle of Being a Caring Behaviour Manager

Valuing individuals

'Education is hanging on until you've caught on.'

Robert Frost

Application

The Powerful Golden Diamond of Behaviour Management Effectiveness

When we combine the two:

First Golden Triangle of Being an Effective Behaviour Manager

and

Second Golden Triangle of Being a Caring Behaviour Manager

we have something that forms the 'Powerful Golden Diamond of Behaviour Management Effectiveness'. This is illustrated on the opposite page. It forms the solid and firm foundation that we can build our effectiveness around. Its solidity is surrounded by, in effect, a multi-faceted framework of surfaces that reflect positivity in the same way that a diamond reflects light from its surfaces. A useful way to help us remember this is shown below, and based on the colours of the rainbow.

RED	ORANGE	YELLOW	GREEN	BLUE	INDIGO	VIOLET
RESPECT	**ORDER**	**YOUNG**	**GOLDEN**	**BOUNDARIES**	**INDIVIDUALS**	**VALUES**
Respecting each individual	Bringing about **O**rder	Displaying firmness, fairness and kindness to all **Y**oung people	The **G**olden Diamond	Setting meaningful **B**oundaries	Motivating **I**ndividuals to learn	**V**aluing individuals

Advice

Look at the Powerful Golden Diamond of Behaviour Management Effectiveness below. With each element of the diamond in place you will have the foundation on which you can develop your skills. How strong is your diamond at the moment?

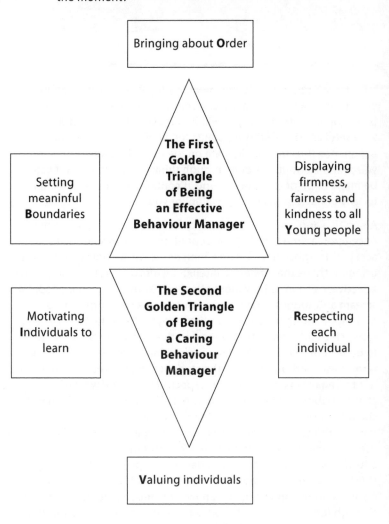

Bringing about Order

The First Golden Triangle of Being an Effective Behaviour Manager

Setting meaninful **B**oundaries

Displaying firmness, fairness and kindness to all **Y**oung people

The Second Golden Triangle of Being a Caring Behaviour Manager

Motivating **I**ndividuals to learn

Respecting each individual

Valuing individuals

The Powerful Golden Diamond of Behaviour Management Effectiveness

Application

9

2 Tips for starters

'Tips for starters' has a double meaning. If you are starting off in education as a new teacher, classroom support assistant, governor, bursar or in another role, you will find these 'tips' very useful. But they are useful as critical starting points for all of us, no matter what our experience thus far. The diagram on the opposite page is here for you to think about. It is only through thinking about it that it can be made to be of relevance to you. It contains essential elements for any behaviour plan you develop for yourself.

A punitive and coercive approach to behaviour management may once upon a time have been accepted, even if it was not really acceptable. Those days are now long gone. We are now charged with using methods that are more intelligent, more acceptable and more effective. As soon as I say more effective, I know that some people will scream and suggest that we are now taking a soft approach to behaviour and that what we do these days is less effective. In reality, research clearly shows that while punitive and cohesive approaches to behaviour management may achieve initial results, in the long term these methods alienate the student from the teacher. We have got to behave in a positive and respectful manner if we wish to change habits and behaviours in others. This is not to imply that there should not be sanctions. But these sanctions should be used as a reminder to students that certain behaviour is not acceptable and not used as a means of retribution. As a key example to students, an educator should be seen as a leader who displays constantly high standards with honourable motives. An educator should find ways to inspire learning and positive behaviour through leadership and not through forcing students to conform to certain rules because they ultimately feel they have little choice.

Advice

Although we will all approach effective behaviour management in our unique way there are certain fundamental principles that should act as a framework for everything we do. With a clear structure to work from we can be confident in our ability to flourish.

 Look at the 'Aspects of tips for starters' below. It is important for all of us to think on how we enable these aspects of effective behaviour management to be part of our natural repertoire. It is also worth thinking about how we would assess ourselves now on a scale of 1 to 3.

- 1 means that we need to consider and develop this skill further.
- 2 means that we are generally effective in this.
- 3 means that we are particularly happy with our skill in this area.

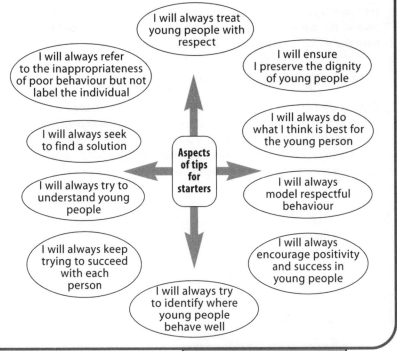

Application

11

Developing the behaviour management plan (1)

We will now look at the development of a behaviour management plan from the point of view of the teacher, but this can easily be adapted to apply to anyone working in a school or college.

STEP 1: the framework of the plan

Remember that this plan is yours. It should reflect what you think and what you feel. You should therefore feel proud of it and have a deep passion for following through what it says. To start you off there are some general principles opposite that should be helpful in guiding you with this ('The plan – framework principles').

You may decide at this stage that you would like to speak to your headteacher/principal to discuss the plan. You will need to ensure that your plan and, in particular, your final sanction, which may involve removing the pupil from the classroom, are in accordance with the school's expectations.

STEP 2: implementation of the plan

Once you have your plan it is important that you are prepared to see it through. Students welcome consistency and they will experience this if you are prepared to carry out the actions in your plan in a consistent way. Try to ensure that you can tick off each of the principles on the opposite page ('The plan – implementation principles').

The plan – framework principles

- My plan has rules that are stated in a positive way and give the students a clear understanding of my expectations. (These rules should be in addition to the school/college rules and not contradict these in any way.)
- My plan gives clear consequences that result from inappropriate behaviour. These should start from consequences for minor and initial misbehaviours and go on to more serious consequences in response to persistent or very serious misbehaviour.
- My plan includes the methods I use to praise students for their positive and appropriate behaviour.

The plan – implementation principles

- My plan is fair. It applies to all students.
- My plan allows for flexibility and humour. I am not on the lookout for misbehaviour.
- My plan involves me identifying the particular and not using generalized comments. If a student misbehaves, I direct them in an assertive way to carry out a particular action.
- My plan allows for an escalation of consequences if my instructions are not followed.
- My plan ensures that I am always in control of my emotions.
- My plan is such that I never have to shout at students. I remain calm as I deal with situations.
- My plan does not allow for any nagging by me. I know this just turns students off.
- My plan includes my being constantly aware of opportunities to praise students.
- My plan includes an understanding of how my own courteous and respectful behaviour influences the behaviour of my students.

'All of life is a constant education.'
Eleanor Roosevelt

Application

Developing the behaviour management plan (2)

STEP 3: techniques for preventing misbehaviour

It seems an obvious point to make but trying to prevent inappropriate behaviour before it happens is preferable to picking up the pieces once it has happened. First, it can save a lot of time and energy, and second, it can lessen the potential for damaged relationships between teacher and student that might initially occur after having to deal with misbehaviour. Preventative measures should therefore be built into the plan. Again, look at the list on the page opposite and decide how many of these techniques you presently have in your plan ('The plan – techniques for preventing misbehaviour').

STEP 4: effective teaching to prevent misbehaviour

There is little doubt that unless students feel interested, motivated and engaged in lessons they will tend to misbehave. Effective teaching is therefore critical in terms of effective classroom behaviour management. For a detailed study of this you can look to either *Effective Teachers* (2002) or *Effective Teachers in Primary Schools* (2003). Both of these show real teachers in their classrooms with an associated analysis of what makes them effective. Beyond pupil management/discipline the Hay McBer Report identified the teaching skills on the opposite page as being critically important for achieving success ('The plan – effective teaching preventing misbehaviour').

STEP 5: influencing behaviour outside the classroom

Many teachers say that their relationship with students improved immensely when they took them on a school trip. The reason for this they feel is that they got to know the students and the students got to know them a lot better. There is a new sense of understanding or empathy. The 'us and them' divide is broken down. The students actually start to like the teacher and will listen more to what the teacher says in the future ('The plan – influencing behaviour outside the classroom').

Advice

The plan – techniques for preventing misbehaviour

- I greet students with a smile at my door ensuring that they are calm before entering my room.
- I have an activity that they are required to do immediately as they enter my room. (A good example of this can be seen on the video accompanying *Effective Teachers* (VITAL 1). This involves Lorraine Biscombe and her technique for having the class chant French words as they enter the class.)
- I have a structured environment in which the students feel safe and secure to operate. Within this I have set procedures for administering basic operations such as collecting in books.
- My room is warm and inviting with interesting and relevant wall displays.

The plan – effective teaching to prevent misbehaviour

- Having high expectations.
- Planning and organizing lessons well. This includes appropriate pace and flow of the lesson.
- Adopting appropriate methods and strategies that suit the needs of the students. This may include VAK (Visual, Auditory and Kinesthetic) inputs to each lesson.
- Paying attention to timing in lessons, together with resource management.
- Carrying out assessments (and giving appropriate feedback).
- Setting appropriate homework.

The plan – influencing behaviour outside the classroom

Examples of influencing behaviour outside of the classroom may be: sport games/matches, trips, the gate at the end of the day, the playground/field, school productions, charity events.

Application

Introducing competence zones

It has already been mentioned that teacher–student relationships can be improved through conversations the teacher has with students around the school. This might be, for example, at break-times or when watching after-school sporting events.

There will be times in your career when you will feel that you have achieved the level of being an expert behaviour manager. At other times you will sink to the bottom of the roller-coaster ride and feel you have lost the plot. The truth is, as in most areas of life, to be found somewhere between these peaks and troughs. The reality is that we must always try to learn, to refresh our ideas and to maintain our belief in the core principles of our philosophy. It is worth looking at the grid opposite that shows what I have called 'Competence Zones'.

Advice

Competence Zones		
1	Unconscious incompetence	As you set off in your work in education you are not aware of what the challenges ahead might be. You don't know what your level of probable needs are – you simply have no conscious awareness of the level of your incompetence. What you are like in this zone will only become apparent once to move to zone 2.
2	Conscious incompetence	You may now have had some experience of life with the students. You swiftly reach an awareness of how much you need to learn. You are fully conscious of feeling incompetent. In this zone you are often unable to easily see how you might advance. You do, however, have a curious mind and a willingness to find out. This is what will lead you through to zone 3.
3	Conscious competence	Now you have reached that state where your actions and behaviours are having a positive impact on the students. You know what you are doing to achieve this and you feel good about it.
4	Unconscious competence	Now you are in automatic mode – autopilot. Things are working well but you may now find it hard to describe to someone else why this is the case. You may hear teachers or other people say things such as 'Well, I just do what I do and it works'.

'No man ever became wise by chance.'

Seneca

Application

Thinking further about competence zones

There are three critically important points to be made about the 'Competence Zones' in education and behaviour management.

1   In your role in education you will probably find that you oscillate between zones at times – even within the course of a day. You might not go back to zone 1 and the 'unconscious incompetence' zone once you have left this but you could find that you jump from zone 4 'unconscious competence' to zone 2 'conscious incompetence'. As long as your life in the 'unconscious competence' zone is working well, things seem to flow. It might even seem easy. But if it starts not to work, you might find suddenly that you go back into the 'conscious incompetence' zone. Try to think why this might be. The reality is that it could be a range of factors, which include those opposite.

2   Living in the 'unconscious competence' zone may have unforeseen dangers and drawbacks. One of these has been mentioned above – in other words if you are merrily going along with things that seem to be working but you are no longer aware of why this is, you may find that suddenly your confidence can be rocked if for some reason your methods no longer work. In addition you might not be flexible enough to adapt to the needs of a range of individuals or groups.

3   There is a greater need now than ever before for all of us to be prepared to mentor and coach others in our school or college. This is difficult to do if we simply say to someone else that we are not sure why our techniques or methods work and we cannot therefore share our ideas. To be able to do this we need to move back into zone 3 and the 'conscious competence' level.

Advice

Look at the explanations below of why an individual may find that they jump from competence zone 4 to competence zone 2. Can you think of other explanations and examples of where this may have happened to you?

	Explanations for the jump from zone 4 to zone 2 for a teacher could include…
1	A new class
2	A new pupil in the class
3	A new classroom
4	A new timetable
5	Personal changes that have impacted on your own mood (illness, children growing up, financial difficulties and so on)
6	Feeling the pressure (of OFSTED!)
7	Feeling the pressure of taking on an additional role in the school/college beyond your present teaching role.
	Three personal examples
1	
2	
3	

However things may go day by day, it is worth remembering that you can always seek to improve on what has already happened. As Margaret Mitchell, from *Gone With the Wind* (1936), said:

'After all, tomorrow is another day'.

Application

3 Effective ways to gain compliance

The following question needs to be asked: 'Does any teacher or anyone in any school want to be liked or would they prefer to be thought of in a negative way by students?' Of course we want to be effective but we can be liked at the same time. Being liked isn't a soft option – quite the opposite in fact. It is hard to achieve and is most definitely not about giving in to unreasonable demands from students or allowing inappropriate behaviour to take place. This would not lead to anybody being liked by students, but would instead simply lead to loss of respect. On the other hand, being liked makes the job of controlling behaviour so much easier. In addition, do we want students to feel that they are self-directed decision makers or do we want them to simply accept what they are told because the consequences are too severe to contemplate? If we want our students to learn how to control their own emotions, behaviour and resultant decisions, then we have got to move beyond the level of simply shouting out instructions and insisting that we are obeyed.

Therefore, in the following methods for gaining the respect and compliance of students we will be looking at how what we do builds personal relationships, gives the student the opportunity to change their own behaviour patterns and helps them to change the way they view things.

Remember

The point is that we can learn to be what we are told we are. This is so powerful in terms of the self-esteem and growth of an individual and the reason why we have got to think about what we say to our students all the time.

Advice

20

The importance of the language we use

Sometimes what appear to be little things can in fact be big things. You may ask what I mean by this. Well, I found that after a number of years of teaching it suddenly dawned on me how important it was to identify the behaviour and not the person. For most of the time we might do this, but without being in zone 3 of 'conscious competence' we can easily make mistakes. Let me give an example. In a class Sam continually calls out. The teacher, in desperation, eventually sends him to the head of year. The head of year herself has had a stressful day and learning about the incident from Sam's teacher tells Sam that he 'is rude, and it will not be tolerated'. On the face of it this might not seem to be too bad. The problem is, however, that Sam's head of year has told Sam he is rude. He 'IS' rude. In other words Sam himself has been labelled with this. It is part of what he is.

'Learning is either a continual thing or it is nothing.'

Frank Tyger

'you ARE lazy'   'you ARE clever'

An alternative approach with Sam and the four NO–NOs

Sam may now in his own mind decide that since he has been told he 'is' rude he will therefore 'be' rude. He is unintentionally given carte blanche to behave in this way. The way to get around this is simply to use different words and to remember that we are identifying the behaviour and not the person. So Sam's head of year could have said 'Sam, this kind of behaviour is unacceptable and I don't expect this from you.' Sam now is given the message that:

1   It is his behaviour that he needs to correct and that if he decides to do so, this is in his control.

2   The head of year has also told him he doesn't expect this from him and therefore he is given the message that this behaviour is not normally part of what he does.

The verbal message we give can really impact strongly on the self-efficacy of the student and the relationship that we develop with them. Some writers, including Thomas McIntyre, have suggested that there are certain words that as educators we should never use with students. McIntyre calls these the 'four NO-NOs'. If we do use the four NO-NO words, we tend to hurt others, blame them, accuse them and create hard feelings that will tend to work against us in the future. We may gain compliance but at a great and unacceptable cost to the student, to us and to our relationship. So let's take a look at the four NO-NOs on the opposite page and then analyse how the four NO-NOs impact on those we might use them with.

Advice

Think about the four NO-NOs below and why we shouldn't use these. You will find the answer in the next few pages but it is good for the moment just to reflect on the danger of using the NO-NOs.

The four NO-NOs	
1	'WHY' questions
2	The word 'YOU'
3	The words 'NO' and 'DON'T'
4	Lecturing/Nagging/Berating

The reason why we should try to eliminate these from our vocabulary is that they tend to make the situation even worse than it was originally.

We will now consider each of these in turn.

Application

1 The 'WHY' NO–NO (why no WHYS?)

To begin with, I should own up: I said to my 14-year-old daughter the other day 'Amy, why you are the most untidy person on this Earth?' as I entered a scene of complete devastation that she calls her bedroom. Immediately I knew this was wrong (particularly as I was then and am now in the process of writing this book!). One part of my mistake we have already discussed: that I was labelling Amy with a particular characteristic that I was saying 'she was'. It wasn't that I was saying she was behaving in an untidy manner that I didn't expect of her (oh, how lovely if this were true!) but I actually said that she, Amy herself, was untidy. In addition I had used the 'WHY' word. In using this I wasn't really expecting to get a reasoned answer, I wasn't really looking for an explanation of the reason for her behaviour, but rather it was me giving her a put-down. It was potentially me starting off a nagging lecture to her. It was me saying I had caught her doing something she shouldn't have done. And it is in many ways the natural action for anyone when they are cornered to find a way out. This could involve fighting back or running away and lying (the 'fight-or-flight' instinct as it is known). We end up forcing them into a situation where their behaviour might be even worse than that we have uncovered.

Such use of the word 'WHY' should therefore be avoided. Our why questions should be reserved for when we are sensitively enquiring about the welfare of a student, perhaps in a counselling situation.

Advice

Think about a situation where you have used language that has told a student that they 'are' something and how this has influenced their future behaviour in this direction.

'Stay interested in everything and everybody. It keeps you young.'
Marie T. Freeman

Remember

Staying interested in people includes being constantly aware ('consciously competent') about what we say to them and how this can impact upon them.

Application

25

2 Why should you not use 'YOU'?

The 'YOU' word should simply be eliminated from our vocabulary when we are dealing with incidents of misbehaviour. Why? (Yes, I used why here, but in a serious and curious way that really is seeking thought from you.) The answer is it is accusing, demeaning and attacking and will simply put the student on the defensive. The interesting point here is to see how we can replace 'YOU' with something else that gives direction but is non-threatening. A good way of doing this is to use an 'I' statement.

So for example:

We can replace: 'Why are you talking?'

With: 'I need quiet in this room now.'

Another example could be:

Replacing: 'You are all behaving stupidly today.'

With: 'Can everyone just think for a moment about the level of noise in the classroom today. Let us start again from here.'

Another useful approach is to use the 'we' statement. When we use this, it helps to give the message that we are in this with the student together. It unites the student with us as the educator.

So for example:

We can replace: 'You are all making such a racket today!'

With: 'Can we all be quiet and respect each other as we take our turn to speak?'

We can also replace 'YOU' with 'US' and 'OUR'.

Advice

Look at the statements below and try to replace the 'YOU' word with other words such as 'I', 'we', 'us' and 'our'.

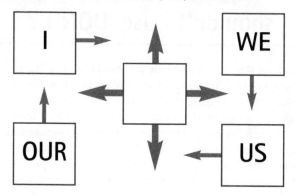

	Replace these
1	'You weren't listening. You're going to end up with no career.'
2	'If I hear you shout one more time, you are in detention.'
3	'You're such a rude person.'
4	'What is wrong with you? You are the worst class I have ever taken. You never open your books when you come into my class.'
5	'How can you be so unpleasant. You always make fun of people who read out in class.'

	These are possible replacements
1	'I want you all to listen carefully to what I am saying so that you can succeed in the way I know you can.'
2	'I like it when I can talk to you quietly and you speak in a similar way to me or anyone else in the class.'
3	'I never like to be spoken to in an unpleasant way. If you speak to me politely, I will always try to help you.'
4	'We have made tremendous progress recently and it is always a great start to a lesson if you get your books out and are ready to start as soon as the lesson begins.'
5	'The great thing about the way that we work together is that each of us respects all the other members of the class.' (Leave it there and let them think about this. This is connected to not nagging which we will look at shortly.)

Application

3 Why no 'NO's, and why shouldn't I use 'DON'T'?

Before we start looking at why we should not use 'NO' or 'DON'T' I will ask you not to think about pink elephants with yellow spots flying through the sky! Please don't think about them. Of course the likelihood is that for the moment you will find it difficult to eliminate this image from your mind. In a similar way, a teacher who shouts at pupils not to run down the corridor might be surprised by the impact of this once they look away. Or should they be surprised? Probably not, because they have in effect directed the attention of the pupils to the idea of running down the corridor. The difficulty is that an instruction like this doesn't give the pupils a clear indication of the type of behaviour you want to see. In addition, you might at times find a teacher carrying out the very kind of behaviour they are insisting should be stopped. So you might have a teacher running down a corridor in order to catch some pupils who are running, or you might hear a teacher yell 'stop shouting' in order to bring quiet into a classroom. A programme on TV just the other night showed a parent hitting an older child because this child had hit his younger brother!

If children are to learn from adults, they need to see the behaviour that is expected of them modelled in the adults. Otherwise very mixed messages are sent out that can confuse everyone.

Remember

Students will learn from the way we model behaviour to them. We want them to inherit a future where they believe you learn by encouraging people to do certain things and modelling this to them. On the other hand, highlighting NOs and DON'Ts can turn students to unwanted behaviours.

Advice

Think about the way that telling a student 'no you can't do that', or 'don't do that' highlights in their mind the very action you are trying to eliminate.

'In a time of drastic change it is the learners who inherit the future.'

Eric Hoffer

Application

4 No nagging? Give it a break man, I love doing this!

You may often hear someone in your school or college who is giving a lecture to a pupil. We may have even done this ourselves at times. Some people seem to actually enjoy lecturing. It may give them a sense of importance and power. The point is that deep down we know that this doesn't work. The reasons for this are clear. Nagging, which in many ways is what the student will think of this, simply makes the person feel they are being talked to in a condescending way. Just as with the examples already given about replacing the word 'YOU' with more effective verbal directives, we need to think of alternatives to nagging.

A key factor is to keep the instruction short. If we don't do this, we can expect a range of responses that will include causing embarrassment, negative self-image and retaliation from defiant students.

Short statements motivate youngsters to:

- think about the limited information
- identify the problem
- devise a solution
- exercise their own initiative and resolve the problem.

For effective behaviour management we need to think of ways of giving an instruction or giving guidance that will allow the person receiving this to make a decision about how they will act on it. These powerful little words used as reminders to students can dissipate potential problem situations that then prevent you from having to use more direct instructions. If the direct instructions are eventually needed, so be it, but as a first move the following are examples of 'little pearls' that should become part of our everyday language and style.

Advice

Consider the examples below of nagging statements and the way they can be replaced by something more effective. Try to think how you would phrase the statement before you look at the replacement examples given.

'John, every time you come in my classroom you have your bag on your back. How many times do I have to tell you? You spend so much time talking to your friends as you come to the lesson that you never think about what you really need to be doing. Don't you ever think?'

'Sarah, every time you start to get bored in the lesson you always start to mess around and start to hit people. You don't always have to show what an idiot you are. Just get on with the work and stop being so stupid.'

	Replacement examples
1	John, bag please!
2	Sarah, if you hit people they won't be your friend.

Remember

Less is often more in terms of giving instructions to students.

Application

More on no nagging and the power of words

No matter what role we have, if in all our interactions with students we model good humour, respect and positivity, we can expect this in return. We are far more likely to gain compliance through desire rather than through the student feeling they have no choice. Life is full of choices and we are therefore offering students the opportunity to practise this in terms of their actions. It may be useful here to put ourselves in the position of being the student and to consider which of the following messages we would feel happier about receiving. Decide for yourself by looking at the examples opposite.

Young people are just like adults. If they think they are being told something that is obvious, by someone who is using a mountain of words to explain it, they will feel they are being spoken to in a condescending way. Less is more in terms of giving guidance to students.

Consider how you would like to be spoken to. Is it statement A or B? Young people are exactly the same as us. They want to be liked and respected even if at times this may not appear to be the case.

Example 1:

1A 'No, you can't do the experiment without wearing goggles.'

1B 'I know you feel uncomfortable with the goggles on but they really are for your own protection.'

Example 2:

2A 'Don't touch that!'

2B 'I'm glad you noticed the displays on the wall. They are brilliant aren't they and all the work of students like you. I ask people not to touch them but rather to look at them so that they stay in a good condition as long as possible.' (*Note this is a longer statement but is highly constructive and engages with the student in a very positive way.*)

Now try to give appropriate messages through the statements you would give in response to the following:

- A student throws a pencil across the room.

- A student hits another student (jokingly) over the head with an exercise book.

- A student is scribbling in their notebook.

- Two students are talking at the back of the class.

Making the problem clear – leaving the solution up to the student

There can be a natural instinct for us as adults to believe that we need to describe in detail *the problem* and *the solution* to the problem when we are talking to students. In fact, we are giving the student a sense of control and empowerment if we simply give a brief comment about something and leave the required action up to the student. We are in the business of trying to develop self-motivated, lifelong learners in education and this approach assists this by allowing them to think and come up with their own solutions. The solutions are then theirs and not considered by them to be imposed upon them. Students learn from the experience even if they sometimes make mistakes in terms of the choices they make. If they do make a mistake, then we can provide a few words of assistance to help them travel along a more desirable route.

Write a note to a student

This is a powerful way of either correcting behaviour or stopping it before it develops into something that may require action. Sticky notes can be used or indeed any other small pieces of paper. Simply written and in a friendly and informative manner, they can be something that the student can act on, rather than them being singled out in front of the rest of the group or class. If this is something that you feel fits with your style, then try it out. If you don't think it will work, then it still might be worth trying at least for a while. Clearly you need to be careful about the way the message is worded as it could be seen by people beyond the student it is directed towards.

Advice

Look at these ways of providing a brief signal that prompts the student(s) to come up with their own solution.

- 'Amal, the water in the beaker has spilled on the bench. What needs to be done now?' (If Amal initially doesn't react to this, you may add a few seconds later 'There are paper towels near the sink Amal.' Again it is important here not to provide the whole solution. Amal must himself decide what to do with the towels. He is still contributing to the solution.)

- 'The bell is going to go in a minute and I haven't yet got all the books in the pile here.'

- 'The room is looking untidy at the moment. Could I have your assistance in the next two minutes to make it more pleasant for us to work in?'

- 'It is great to have so many enthusiastic answers but what do we do first?' (Expecting hands to be raised first.)

Now consider the kinds of messages that you might write on sticky notes or small pieces of paper to give to individual students or groups. How would the following work for you?

- 'Pip, can you always put your hand up before giving an answer?'

- 'John, I heard about the sad news in your family. If you wish to speak to me, please do so after the lesson.'

- 'You gave brilliant answers in the lesson today. Can I have a quick word with you after the lesson.'

- 'Kauser, I was aware of you talking a lot in the class today. This is not like you. I expect more concentration tomorrow.'

A lasting and glorious impact

Our intention as adults must be to want students to take on a responsible role that will help to guide them through their lives. We don't want them to grow up in a world where they think that they simply accept what they are told. We don't want that in lessons nor should we want it in terms of the way they react to developing as responsible citizens. A moment's thought will tell us how dangerous giving them the idea that they should simply accept things they are told could be with gang leaders, drug dealers and even terrorists – such people are all too happy to steer unquestioning and malleable young minds.

A genuine sense of cooperation in our schools and colleges will bring about an ethos where behaviour is the desired and accepted norm by everybody, and this then breeds an atmosphere where teaching is a joy and learning is a privilege. This may prove to be something that challenges us during busy and hard days where students really do demand an awful lot of us. It must nevertheless be our constant aim. We are told that about 80 per cent of the way a child behaves comes from their home. My experience as a teacher and behaviour leader in schools has certainly confirmed this for me. But equally, schools do make a difference. In the various roles I have had in filming teachers and leaders in schools, and in a regional role where I have visited hundreds of schools and colleges, I have seen the impact that schools, colleges and individuals within these schools and colleges can have in terms of positively impacting on the life chances of young people.

The wonderful educators that we find all around us (and we all aspire to be) treat each individual with respect, courtesy and dignity and never lose faith in the fact that people can develop and grow. They never lose belief in the fact that each individual can succeed given the opportunity to do so. You and I can be like these people. We can be wonderful educators if we want to be.

Think about the qualities of those educators you have known who made a big difference in your life. What qualities did they have and what did they say to you that made you feel good about yourself and be able to achieve in your life? Clearly these are the attributes we need to model with all our students.

Key qualities:

- The key to success for us as behaviour managers, behaviour coaches and effective educators.
- The key to success for us as human beings interacting with all other human beings.

Your ideas may include the following.

They were always:

- kind
- understanding
- patient
- respectful.

They always made me feel:

- I was capable of achieving a lot
- that taking risks was OK
- that my ideas were valuable
- that they liked me.

You will be able to think of many other ideas. It is worth making a note of them here as a reminder.

'Anyone who stops learning is old, whether at twenty or eighty.'
Henry Ford

Application

4 Praising positive behaviour

The following may be hard to accept if we are stuck in certain ways of thinking about behaviour management. These thoughts may include the belief that effective behaviour management is about a series of strategies that simply (though in reality it is never simple and far from it) enable us to correct unwanted behaviour. This may principally involve a series of punitive measures that show the student that they have committed a crime that they must pay the penalty for. Clear sanctions need to be part of our overall strategy, but wouldn't it be nice if we could be in a position where these have only to be used in extreme cases? The reality is that this is possible and the strategy we are going to look at is both simple and really does work. How do we know this? Well research tells us that it does. So what is this thing, this magical solution? Well it is no magical solution but it definitely works.

It involves our catching the students being good and rewarding them for this. The rewards do not have to be big – but they will have an incredible impact. It could simply be a smile, a thank you or a thumbs-up. You may decide that you want to go beyond this and make the praise more formal with 'positive points', small prizes, or leaving the classroom first at the end of a lesson. The secret ingredient that is essential and goes with the action is that the student must perceive that we are genuine with this. We will then be acting in a proactive way rather than a reactive way and, as a result, will both feel that we are in control and actually be in control. And the control will make us feel good because it is achieved in a way that pleases the student, builds their self-esteem and at the same time makes them feel positive about us. Don't let people tell you that this is being soft. This is not being soft but simply using a technique that works because it locks into how we all like to feel as human beings.

Advice

As human beings we respond to praise. We may find it difficult to find the time and energy to praise young people when we are faced with examples of misbehaviour. It is a challenge that we should face if we seek to be effective as behaviour coaches.

On every staffroom wall there should be a notice saying

'Catch them being good today.'

The challenge should go out to everyone to see how many times they can do this in a meaningful way. Try to think how you do this now and can do it even more in the future. Here are three steps that you will find helpful.

Step 1   The first step in the process is to give the young person some indication of the type of behaviour we are expecting to see.

Step 2   After this we must make every attempt to give praise whenever we observe the desirable behaviour. We mustn't be looking for perfection but rather a movement towards the final state we are seeking. We should reward the desired behaviour immediately so that the student sees a direct correlation between the behaviour they are now displaying and our pleasure in the efforts they are making.

Step 3   As time goes by we can start to give praise more sparingly yet still making the student perfectly aware that we are looking for the desired outcome. We might also now be looking for a greater degree of accuracy.

Application

Potential problems with positive reinforcement techniques

The techniques mentioned on pages 38–39 do work. Try them and see the results for yourself. You will see them employed by some effective teachers who are unaware at times that this is what they are doing. Effectiveness doesn't happen by magic, however, and when analysed it is possible to see what the building blocks of any effective teacher's actions comprise of and one of these skills will be the use of positive reinforcement. However, like most things in life, there can be certain drawbacks to using 'catch them being good' techniques that we should consider here. In doing this we can then make sure that our awareness can help to prevent such drawbacks from happening.

Think for one minute before looking at the suggestions below and decide what you think the drawbacks might be.

OK, so now you have thought about this, compare your ideas with those below.

1   Giving gifts as prizes for positive behaviour may give the message to students that they need only do something if they are rewarded. It may breed materialistic views that include WIIFM (What's In It For Me?).

2   We are seeking an inner motivation and decision making that external rewards may not encourage. Looking for and seeking external approval for their behaviour may encourage students to give less consideration to their inner worth and self-esteem.

3   Students who are not offered rewards may react poorly if they feel they have contributed positive behaviour. This will particularly be the case if a few students with exceptional behaviour always win the prizes.

4   Some students are reluctant to be labelled with 'being good'.

Advice

Trying to avoid the problems associated with positive reinforcement techniques as mentioned opposite is important. Here are some suggestions to help you.

1   We may start off giving material awards, but always accompany these with human expressions of a smile, a brief word or a nod. We can then slowly replace the material awards with just the human expressions.

2   We should always identify and comment on the positive behaviour and not the students themselves. Students find this more acceptable and easier to manage. It is also important to be specific. This tells the student that you really are observing them and not just giving a global 'you've worked well today' type of comment.

3   We should link praise to positive aspects of a person's endeavours. Effort (but be specific where the effort was observed) is worth a lot of praise. We need to consider how much we are praising attainment and how much we are praising achievement. The balance should be shifted towards praising achievement.

4   We should always express high expectations. It is amazing how much, as human beings, we tend to live up to what people tell us.

Remember

1 People appreciate that rewards don't always cost anything.

2 Always refer to behaviour.

3 Try to praise achievement more than attainment.

4 Always express high expectations.

Application

5 Using teaching styles to impact on behaviour

There are very few statements in this world that can be said with absolute certainty but perhaps one of them is that,

there is an inextricable link between effective teaching and effective behaviour management.

Without one it is not possible to have the other in a way that is sustainable. In addition, without effective behaviour management and effective teaching we will not provide the right environment for effective learning to take place. It is for this reason that we will now look at some of the essential characteristics of effective teaching.

If students are bored in lessons, they will feel there is no return for any investment they may make. They will not feel that they want to contribute to preserving what is going on because they cannot see any reason for doing so. In simple terms there is no WIIFM (What's In It For Me?) that they can detect. They will then make up their own entertainment to try to fill the time. This will almost inevitably result in many of the characteristics of what we call 'misbehaviour'. In 1989, 'The Elton Report' stated that 'Teachers in our survey were most concerned about the cumulative effects of disruption to their lessons caused by relatively trivial but persistent misbehaviour.' The report highlights that this kind of behaviour might typically consist of the behaviours listed opposite.

Advice

Many of the ongoing and small but wearing features of misbehaviour in classrooms can be minimized by effective teaching styles. Understanding the components of effective teaching will therefore make us better behaviour coaches.

 The Elton Report said that the following relatively trivial behaviours bother teachers most. Do they bother you?

	Regularly bother me
Talking out of turn	
Calculated idleness	
Hindering other pupils	
Not being punctual	
Making unnecessary non-verbal noise	
Persistently infringing class rules	
Getting out of their seat without permission	
Verbal abuse towards other pupils	
General rowdiness, horseplay or mucking about	
Cheeky remarks	
Physical aggression towards other pupils	
Physical destructiveness	

The Elton Report added that this may then move into very direct challenges to the teachers consisting of:

- verbal abuse to the teacher;
- physical aggressiveness towards the teacher.

Application

43

Effective teaching helping to combat trivial misbehaviour

Effective teaching can help to eliminate trivial behaviour problems in the majority of cases. Most students have the attitude that they will respond positively in lessons if they respect the teacher, but if they don't, then they will misbehave. Often when they leave the class after causing disruption, students will comment and complain that 'the lesson was boring, they never get any work done, and the teacher can't control us'. Effective teachers will not have these accusations held against them.

It is therefore worth looking at the aspects of our own teaching skills on the opposite page and grading ourselves on a scale of 1 to 3.

- Grade 1 means that we need to consider and develop this skill further.
- Grade 2 means that we are generally effective in this.
- Grade 3 means that we are particularly happy with our skill in this area.

Try to grade yourself now and then at two weeks and four weeks later.

Teaching skills grid				
	How I grade myself now	Teaching skill	How I grade myself two weeks later	How I grade myself four weeks later
1		I greet the students as they enter my classroom.		
2		I have prepared an activity for the students to start working on as soon as they enter my classroom		
3		The main body of my lesson is well structured.		
4		I am interested in the work I am doing with students and demonstrate this enthusiasm to them.		
5		I vary the inputs to my lessons to engage the students in different ways.		
6		I am conscious of students accessing information in a variety of ways (VAK).		
7		I ensure the lessons are both challenging and enjoyable		
8		I ensure that I involve all students in each lesson.		
9		I have differentiation in my lessons.		
10		I give lots of praise and am aware of catching students being good.		
11		I refer to students by their names.		
12		I ensure that there is pace and flow in my lessons.		
13		I have resources in my lessons at hand for ease of access and use.		
14		I always give the clear message that my expectations of students are high.		
15		I am flexible in my lessons, being able to change the plan if I perceive this is in the best interest of the students.		
16		I show respect for students at all times.		
17		I bring the lesson to a close with a well-structured plenary.		

Application

Using the Hay McBer Report Model

If you wish to look into characteristics of effective teaching in more detail, it is worth looking at the Hay McBer Report (2000). This gives a useful analysis that acts as a framework for considering our own teaching. A Model of Teacher Effectiveness looks at the effectiveness of teachers by dividing the analysis into three key elements. These are:

1 Teaching skills
2 Professional characteristics
3 Classroom climate.

The report then subdivides teaching skills into seven categories as follows:

A High expectations
B Planning
C Methods and strategies
D Pupil management/discipline
E Time and resource management
F Assessment
G Homework.

In addition, the Hay McBer Report says that teaching skills can be observed in terms of:

1 The way the lesson is structured and flows.
2 The number of pupils on task through the course of the lesson.

Advice

The Report further subdivides professional characteristics into five clusters of characteristics as follows:

Professional characteristics		
	Cluster	*Characteristics*
A	Professionalism	• Challenge and support • Confidence • Creating trust • Respect for others
B	Thinking	• Analytical thinking • Conceptual thinking
C	Planning and setting expectations	• Drive for improvement • Information seeking • Initiative
D	Leading	• Flexibility • Holding people accountable • Managing pupils • Passion for learning
E	Relating to others	• Impact and influence • Teamworking • Understanding others

Referring to the clusters of professional characteristics, the Hay McBer Report says that, 'effective teachers need to have some strengths in each of them'. Realizing and recognizing the distinctive nature of each teacher, the report makes it clear that:

'Effective teachers show distinctive combinations of characteristics that create success for their pupils'.

Application

The Hay McBer Report and classroom climate

The Hay McBer Report also subdivides classroom climate into nine dimensions as follows:

		Professional characteristics
A	Participation	Clarity around the purpose of each lesson. How each lesson relates to the broader subject, as well as clarity regarding the aims and objectives of the school.
B	Order	Order within the classroom, where discipline, order and civilized behaviour are maintained.
C	Standards	A clear set of standards as to how pupils should behave and what each pupil should do and try to achieve, with a clear focus on higher rather than minimum standards.
D	Fairness	The degree to which there is an absence of favouritism, and a consistent link between rewards in the classroom and actual performance.
E	Participation	The opportunity for pupils to participate actively in the class by discussion, questioning, giving out materials and other similar activities.
F	Support	Feeling emotionally supported in the classroom, so that pupils are willing to try new things and learn from mistakes.
G	Safety	The degree to which the classroom is a safe place, where pupils are not at risk from emotional bullying, or other fear-rousing factors.
H	Interest	The feeling that the classroom is an interesting and exciting place to be, where pupils feel stimulated to learn.
I	Environment	The feeling that the classroom is a comfortable, well organized, clean and attractive physical environment.

Advice

The Hay McBer Report says that teaching skills and professional characteristics are factors that relate to what a teacher brings to the job. Look at the descriptions of teaching skills and professional characteristics on the previous pages and then decide what your understanding of the difference might be.

The Hay McBer Report says: 'Whilst teaching skills can be learned, sustaining these behaviours over the course of a career will depend on the deeper seated nature of professional characteristics.'

 What do you think the nature of professional characteristics might be?

The Hay McBer Report says: 'Professional characteristics are deep-seated patterns of behaviour which outstanding teachers display more often, in more circumstances and to a greater degree of intensity than effective colleagues. They are how the teacher does the job, and have to do with self-image and values; traits, or the way the teacher habitually approaches situations; and at the deepest level, the motivation that drives performance.'

 Classroom climate is referred to as an output measure. What do you think this means?

The Hay McBer Report says: Classroom climate is what the teacher creates through teaching skills and professional characteristics and it is what influences the pupils to learn.

The Hay McBer Report says: Teachers are not clones and there are a number of ways that a teacher can achieve effectiveness:
'There is, in other words, a multiplicity of ways in which particular characteristics determine how a teacher chooses which approach to use from a repertoire of established techniques in order to influence how pupils feel.'

Applying the same methods that we previously used to consider our current level of teaching skills, we will assess our group skills both for now (and in the future) using the grid below. You might find it interesting to come back to the grid after two weeks and after four weeks to look at how you have reflected and perhaps adapted the way you approach managing groups. To be effective in our efforts to improve through being reflective practitioners, we need to be honest with ourselves in our self-assessments. To do this it might be worth focusing on a particular group that you teach which might provide you with challenges.

	My grade now	Group skills grid – part A	Two weeks later	Four weeks later
		Teaching skill		
1		I am aware of the individuals in the group and the roles they play in the group.		
2		I am aware of the group identity.		
3		I use all opportunities to get to know, and understand more, the individuals in the group. In this way I actively use all opportunities to connect more with the group.		
4		I greet individuals when they enter the classroom.		
5		I always talk to individuals and the group with respect.		
6		I involve the class in an activity as soon as they enter the classroom.		
7		I am aware that others will follow the leader and I therefore make efforts to involve and engage the leader.		
8		I involve groups within the group in learning activities.		
9		I am always catching individuals, small groups and the whole group being good and I use rewards.		
10		I never embarrass through nagging any individual within a group in front of the group or others.		

Advice

Getting groups to behave might seem like a challenge but if we follow certain guidelines we should find the job a lot easier.

Group skills grid – part B				
	My grade now	**Teaching skill**	**Two weeks later**	**Four weeks later**
11		I always try to make my lessons interesting.		
12		I relate to the life experiences and interests of the individuals and the group in my lessons.		
13		I smile and laugh with the class.		
14		I determine any reasons for misbehaviour before I react to them.		
15		I use low-key interventions in the first instance to try to avoid an escalation of the unwanted behaviour, before I move through a structured system that I have predetermined.		
16		I show interest in the students and their work at all times.		
17		I always refer to behaviour and not individuals. I do not label students but rather refer to their actions.		
18		I structure lessons so that there is challenge for individuals, groups and the whole class.		
19		I have high expectations that encourage and stretch the group in a meaningful and achievable way.		
20		I never carry anything that is not positive and might have happened in one lesson over into another lesson.		

'The man who is too old to learn was probably always too old to learn.'

Henry S. Haskins

Remember

Many of the ways that we effectively deal with individuals are the same as the ways that we effectively deal with groups.

Application

7 How to deal with bullying

Any one who has endured bullying will know that the pain and the scars from the experience can last a long time, if not forever. Bullying is not something that just happens to children; on 28 November 1996, the Institute of Personnel and Development (IPD) published the results of a survey revealing that one in eight (around three million) UK employees have been bullied at work in the previous five years. Over half of those who have experienced bullying say it is commonplace in their organization and a quarter say it has got worse in the last year. As educationalists, we may not wish to admit it, but we may have felt bullied by young people. No one should have to put up with the torture of bullying. As educationalists and coaches of positive behaviour, we need to equip ourselves with the techniques and skills that can be employed to counter any instances of bullying that we witness. In order to do this we need to be clear about what bullying actually is.

Defining bullying

We might describe bullying as 'the tormenting of others through verbal *harassment*, physical *assault*, or other more subtle methods of *coercion* such as *manipulation*'. This is the definition given in Wikipedia, the free encyclopedia on the internet.

Bullying is ongoing and bullies use aggression or the threat of it to gain control over others. It is common that bullies will target individuals that they perceive to be weaker than themselves in some way. This could be because they are younger, less physically developed, or have a more limited verbal ability, and as a result they present an easy target or victim who is then unable to respond in an assertive manner to the attack they experience.

Advice

As effective behaviour coaches we will be in a strong position to take action to eliminate all forms of bullying. The satisfaction that this will bring us is immense; the relief it will bring to victims of bullying could be life-changing.

 Q1. The definition of bullying on the previous page includes the words *harassment, assault, coercion* and *manipulation.* Try to give your own meaning to these terms before looking at the definitions below.

 Q2. What type of bullying would you expect to occur most often when adults are not around?

 Q3. How does the bullying change when adults are around?

A1 The following definitions should be useful.

- Harassment – offensive behaviour that can take many forms.

- Assault – a crime of violence against another person. Technically speaking, in England, Wales and the United States assault is the threat of violence, whereas the actual violence itself is called 'battery'.

- Coercion – the practice of compelling a person to involuntarily behave in a certain way. Coercion may involve threats or intimidation or some other form of pressure or force. There may be physical or psychological harm involved.

- Manipulation – when a person or group seeks to control another person or group by unfair means for their own advantage.

A2 When adults are not present to prevent or stop it, bullying will often take on a physical form of '*direct bullying*'.

A3 If adults are present but distant, the bullying tends to take a verbal form of intimidation and condescension. If the adult is near, this can become more subtle still with non-verbal bullying. Both of these can be referred to as '*indirect bullying*'.

Application

Knowing some of the facts about bullying

Childline (www.childline.org.uk, tel: 0800 1111) has counselled nearly two million children and young people. The main problems children contacted Childline about from April 2004 to March 2005 were:

- bullying (23 per cent of calls);
- family issues (12 per cent);
- physical abuse (9 per cent);
- concern for others (7 per cent);
- facts of life (7 per cent);
- sexual abuse (6 per cent).

So bullying tops the list of concerns that children have. In addition, Childline found that most children (63 per cent) who called about bullying said that they were bullied in school.

In a survey that it conducted through the Thomas Coram Research Unit at the Institute of Education in 2003, Childline found:

- Just over half of both primary (51 per cent) and secondary school (54 per cent) pupils thought that bullying was 'a big problem' or 'quite a problem' in their school.
- Just over half (51 per cent) of Year 5 pupils reported that they had been bullied during the term, compared with just over a quarter (28 per cent) of Year 8 pupils. Considerable variation was reported in the level of bullying between schools.
- Girls were almost as likely as boys to have been bullied in both age groups. In Year 8, a higher proportion of Black and Asian pupils (33 per cent) reported that they had been bullied, compared with pupils of other ethnic groups (30 per cent) or white pupils (26 per cent).

On the previous page I mentioned that bullying can take on a *'direct'* or *'indirect'* form. Look at the page opposite and think about the forms of direct and indirect bullying that you have observed in your school/college over the past month.

Advice

These forms of *direct bullying* are most often observed in male bullies.	
Direct bullying	**Observed or uncovered**
Shoving and poking	
Throwing things	
Slapping	
Choking	
Punching and kicking	
Stabbings	
Pulling hair	
Scratching	
Biting	

These forms of *indirect bullying* are most often observed in male bullies.	
Indirect bullying	**Observed or uncovered**
Name calling	
The silent treatment	
Arguing others into submission	
Manipulation	
Gossip/false gossip	
Lies	
Rumours/false rumours	
Staring	
Giggling, laughing at the victim	
Saying certain words that trigger a reaction from a past event	
Mocking	

Application

Knowing bullies

If we are to deal with bullies and instances of bullying, we need to be aware of the signs that suggest that a child might be a bully. To assist with this, you can use the checklist on the opposite page for a variety of characteristics you might see in potential bullies

There is a lot of evidence to suggest that if aggressive behaviour is not challenged in childhood, there is a danger that it may become habitual. It is also likely that bullying during childhood puts children at risk of criminal behaviour and domestic violence in adulthood. This reinforces still further the need for all of us to deal with bullying effectively. If we believe in the spirit of *Every Child Matters* and that every child really does matter, then dealing effectively with bullying has got to be a high priority.

Advice

Think about a student that you know who you either suspect is a bully or you might be fairly certain is a bully. See how many of the boxes you can tick as 'observed' that describe this student's behaviour and characteristics.

	Observed
Lacks empathy and concern for others	
Has difficulty conforming to rules	
Is defiant and aggressive towards adults and authority figures – adults may be frightened of the bully	
Is hot-tempered, easily angered, impulsive and has a low frustration tolerance	
Teases others in a hurtful manner	
Picks on others who are weaker; this is not done in self-defence	
Intimidates others through threats or reputation	
Commits acts of physical aggression – may be physically bigger and stronger than their victims	
Has strong needs to dominate and control their peers	
Is a boy (Boys are more likely than girls to be bullies. However, girls are more likely to engage in 'sneakier' forms of harassment.)	
Is good at talking themselves out of situations	
Engages in other antisocial behaviours	
Is less popular (particularly primary school pupils)	
Has negative attitudes towards school and gets lower grades	

Knowing victims

Once again, to be effective in dealing with bullying we need to be aware of the familiar characteristics of the victims of bullies. Evidence suggests that those who are victims of bullying are typically anxious, insecure, cautious and suffer from low self-esteem, rarely defending themselves or retaliating when confronted by others who bully them. They may lack social skills and friends and are therefore often socially isolated. Victims may be close to their parents and may have parents who can be described as overprotective. The major physical characteristic of victims is that they tend to be weaker than their peers; other physical characteristics – such as weight, dress or wearing eyeglasses – do not appear to be significant factors that can be correlated with victimization.

Victims of bullying can be classified as 'passive' or 'proactive'. Passive victims will do nothing to provoke a bully but they are still singled out for the bully's treatment. They will often end up giving in to the demands of the bully.

Proactive victims tend to be socially unskilled youngsters who irritate other children. This behaviour stimulates others to pick on them. Also, since proactive victims provoke incidents, others (both children and adults) often feel that the attacks are justified. Proactive victims are commonly diagnosed with ADHD (attention deficit hyperactivity disorder). It is believed that the hyperactivity is a contributing factor to the irritating nature of their behaviour.

Bullying is ongoing and bullies use aggression or the threat of it to gain control over others. It is common that bullies will target individuals that they perceive to be weaker than themselves in some way. This could be because they are younger, less physically developed, or have a more limited verbal ability, and as a result they present an easy target or victim who is then unable to respond in an assertive manner to the attack they experience.

Victims need to learn how to seek help from adults. They may also need to improve their social skills to assist them in making friends.

Advice

Think about a student that you know who you either suspect is being bullied or you are fairly certain is bullied. See how many of the boxes under 'observed' you can tick that describe this student's behaviour and characteristics.

	Observed
Personal characteristics	
Underdeveloped social skills	
Shyness or lack of assertiveness	
Few or no friends	
Never or infrequently invited to parties/gatherings of other children	
Small physical stature	
Physical evidence of bullying	
Missing belongings	
Missing money, or what would be bought with those funds	
Unexplained bruises, cuts and abrasions	
Torn, bloodied or dirtied clothing	
Behaviours	
Feigning illness to avoid environments where bullies are present	
Fear of going to school	
Skipping school or cutting certain classes/activities	
Not eating lunch	
Sadness/depression	
Nightmares	
Drop in grades	
Carrying weapons	

Application

How we can help victims in school

Every member of a school team can help the victims of bullying. We all have a part to play. Now that we are armed with our understanding of what bullying is and an awareness of the characteristics of bullies and their victims, there are some fairly simple steps that we can take . Clearly this will work most effectively if the following suggestions are part of a school/college policy on dealing with bullying, that everyone understands. Are the following steps part of the understood process for assisting the victims of bullying in your school/college?

1   If a person voluntarily comes to you for help, then they need to be listened to. Sometimes this is all that the victim wants and needs.

2   After investigating the situation, it may be that intervention is necessary. The situation needs to be addressed and hopefully a resolution to the problem can be found.

3   Inform the parents of the victim and of the bully. Discuss possible solutions with them. Arrange a meeting with them if possible.

4   Follow up by communicating with the victim, the parents and the teachers about the situation.

5   Monitor the behaviour of the bully and the safety of the victim on a school-wide basis.

6   Teach kids how to stand up to bullies and learn how to defend themselves. This is about being assertive.

How we can help to limit instances of bullying

The ideal of course would be to prevent bullying happening in the first place. This is something we can at least aspire towards. Being proactive about this can limit a lot of pain and anguish for all those concerned in an incidence of bullying. It can also prevent a lot of unnecessary time and energy being employed in the school/college in trying to pick up the pieces and repair situations once they have occurred. Look at the page opposite and reflect on how your school/college tries to limit any situations of bullying.

Advice

Place ticks in the boxes below to indicate the proactive measures your school/college already employs to limit incidents of bullying. What can you do about any gaps? Are there other measures you can think of?

	Part of our bullying policy
We make all adults aware of the nature of bullying situations and involve them in combatting these	
We make it clear that bullying is never acceptable	
We have held a school conference day devoted to bully/victim problems	
We treat supervision in the playground, corridors and washrooms with vigilance	
We emphasize caring, respect and safety	
We emphasize consequences of hurting others	
We enforce consistent and immediate consequences for aggressive behaviours	
We follow up on all instances of aggression	
We treat communication among school administrators, teachers, parents and students as vitally important	
We have a school problem box where students can report problems, concerns and offer suggestions	
We teach cooperative learning activities	
We help bullies with anger control and the development of empathy	
We encourage positive peer relations	
We offer a variety of extracurricular activities which appeal to a range of interests	

Application

Setting up school systems

On the opposite page is a brief questionnaire about bullying that you could adapt for use in your school/college. This could form the first stage of a strategy that you might help to set up to deal with bullying. Ultimately, the strategy and system should involve all the school/college community, parents, carers and the wider community. Raising awareness is vitally important. The school should be open about the facts of bullying; giving such facts can be powerful in terms of combatting bullying.

The steps you take may include the following:

Step 1 Set up a committee within the school to constantly review the way that the school approaches bullying. This could consist of pupils, support staff, teachers and parents.

Step 2 After a period of gaining knowledge about the level of bullying in the school and reviewing the information available on dealing with bullying, the committee should decide on an anti-bullying programme. This should fit the particular needs of the setting.

Step 3 Awareness-raising events could be organized where the local community is invited in to the school. In this way, staff, parents/carers, local businesses and the local community are all given information that can help them to take positive action against bullying.

Step 4 Particular times of the day when bullying does or can occur should be investigated and action taken to reduce the potential occurrence. This might include greater supervision at these times.

Step 5 It has already been mentioned that informing parents is critical in successfully combatting bullying. Parents need to be kept informed about the anti-bullying programme the school is employing and how they can support this.

Steps like these might not remove bullying all together but will certainly raise awareness and understanding, and work towards reducing cases of bullying.

Advice

Here is a questionnaire you might like to use in your school/college. First have a go yourself. In the box beside each statement simply write 'T' if you believe the statement is true and 'F' if you believe it is false. Then check your answers with those on page 88. These are based on evidence in Canada and you can find out more about this at www.bullybeware.com

Reasons why we must take action against bullying

	T or F
By age 24, 60 per cent of identified bullies have a criminal conviction	
Children who are repeatedly victimized sometimes see suicide as their only escape	
Schools are a prime location for bullying	
Bullies lose their popularity as they get older and are eventually disliked by the majority of students	
Primary-age children who were labelled by their peers as bullies required more support as adults from government agencies, had more court convictions, more alcoholism, more antisocial personality disorders and used more mental health services	
Many adults do not know how to intervene in bullying situations, therefore bullying is often overlooked	
Bullying occurs once every seven minutes	
On average, bullying episodes are brief, approximately 37 seconds long	
The emotional scars from bullying can last a lifetime	
The majority of bullying occurs in or close to school buildings	
Most victims are unlikely to report bullying	
Only 25 per cent of students report that teachers intervene in bullying situations	
While 71 per cent of teachers believe they always intervene	

Application

8 Using humour as an effective tool

Humour is very powerful. Some of the very best teachers I have had the pleasure to watch use humour to connect with a class in a deep and meaningful way. We will therefore look at why humour can be employed to impact on behaviour and how it works as a powerful tool in behaviour management.

There is a lot of evidence about how humour can be used as an effective leadership tool, in a variety of work situations. The techniques that work for us in our interactions as adults apply equally to the way we build relationships with students. It has been found that humour:

- facilitates communication;
- relieves stress;
- conveys information well and draws attention to it.

In difficult behavioural situations, humour can be used by us to communicate and express instructions in a way that is not offensive or threatening. Expressed in another way the same message may be perceived by the student as a reprimand. It is important that signals beyond the verbal message such as physical gestures, a smile and the tone of voice all allow the student to know that for the moment the normal rules of behaviour do not apply. In this way, through humour, we can indicate that we are 'just playing' and this allows both us and the student the space to act out resolving the situation in the knowledge that we can move back into a different mode of behaviour if things don't work out well. The use of humour gives speakers the right to deny that they meant anything by their comments and it gives listeners the right to act as if nothing hasbeen conveyed. Humour therefore gives both speaker and listener a powerful 'get-out clause' if they decide that the communication just isn't having the kind of impact they had intended.

Advice

The power of humour in leadership and in dealing with behaviour is something that no one should ignore. Used appropriately it will build relationships in a way that can surprise us.

 When using humour to communicate in difficult situations, ask yourself three questions.

1   Do the non-verbal signals clearly convey that the comment is intended as a joke?
2   Will the form of humour leave the student in a good mood (for example, by avoiding negative, aggressive humour)?
3   Is the humour calling attention to something valuable (for example, the correct behaviour, rather than the mistake itself)?

Bearing these points in mind, look at the situations below and think of suitable humorous comments that could be effective.

1	You are taking a class to the hall. They come out in a rowdy mood making a lot of noise.
2	You are about to begin a lesson and find that the class are making so much noise that you may have to shout over the top of the noise to get them to hear your instruction.
3	You have asked the class to rinse out the beakers at the end of a science lesson. John has spent five minutes at the sink rinsing out the same beaker.
4	You dramatically stop, say 'sshh' and ask the class to listen putting your hand to your ear. They stop talking. You say 'Oh, thank goodness for that, now I know I have brought the right class with me. I was worried for a moment.' The class smile and walk along quietly from here on.
5	You walk up to Peter on a front row table and ask him if he has brought his microphone and loudspeaker along with him so that you can speak to the class. He and students near him laugh – this is heard by other students and spreads through the class so that their attention is on you again.
6	'Well John, I have to say that if a job is worth doing it is worth doing well. You have won top prize for the cleanest beaker of the year award. It is probably good to stop now though before you rinse your fingers down the sink.'

Application

Why humour?

The simple answer to this question is that research tells us it works. Humour puts people in a good mood, which tends to make us feel more cooperative and less inclined to want to be in conflict with others. This applies both to us and to the pupils with whom we are interacting. Humour seems to allow people to come to a collective understanding that a situation is safer and less serious than it would first appear. There is a lot of evidence to suggest that people who watch humorous films tend to react better to subsequent stressful situations.

We have got to be open to allowing humour to come from the students as well. Our ability to 'take a joke' also opens an important channel for students to communicate with us and at times to give valuable feedback. Humour is also a generous act when it is given to others in the right spirit. It says to someone that you like and value them and want to share a good time with them. It is then something that is uplifting, positive and respectful. As we are modelling effective strategies for dealing with potential conflict, using humour should be part of the coaching techniques we demonstrate to other adults and students.

Humour can be an excellent way to capture the attention of students. One way in which humour is often used effectively is within anecdotal illustrations. As educators we should always be on the lookout for developing stories that we can use with students. The stories themselves may not fully illustrate the point you are making but they can be an excellent way of building bridges and bringing the message we wish to relay far nearer home for the student. And finally, another valuable use of humour in teaching is to laugh at yourself. We all make mistakes – this is part of what living and growing is all about. When we can see the humour in what we have done, we put the students at ease and also maintain our own composure and confidence.

Advice

Now it is your turn. You may wish to discuss the following with your colleagues to arrive at suitable responses with appropriate wording. If you practise these first, more ad-lib responses will become natural to you. It can even become great fun. So try out the situations given below.

1 A student swears at another student.
2 A student leaves the class to go to the toilet and takes a long time to return.
3 A student is tapping on the table at the back of the room.
4 A student fails to do homework for the second time.
5 A student is looking out of the window – for some time!

Remember

You may need to coach other adults in the school who believe that using humour as a behaviour tool is just a cop-out. This is something that needs as much thought as the way we actually use humour with our students.

'What I want to achieve', and motivations for behaviour

We have chosen to enter a profession that is high octane, demanding and, at times, stressful. But the personal rewards are great. We perform with the adrenaline and energy of an actor on the stage each day and our performance is being assessed by some of the harshest critics – the students themselves. Most of them will want to go along with what is being offered as long as they can see a return for their investment. They need to be sure that what is being offered to them matches their needs. They need to be certain that the school or college is there to support them. They want to achieve results that help them to move forward in their lives but within a framework that is helping them to grow as individuals. They want us to help them develop as lifelong learners who can respond to the ever-changing world that we live in. They will want to be able to sense the moral purpose behind the way the school/college operates. Students themselves may not articulate these views in this way but they will certainly sense the true motives of the school/college and the people who work in it, and they will respond to this.

We need to constantly reflect on what we want to achieve and this should match the needs of the students (see above). It is very easy to lose sight of this when we are dealing with a series of circumstances that can appear to act against us. These may include the following:

- A complex timetable that places high demands on us with little time for reflection and professional development.

- Pressures of achieving externally, and sometimes internally, imposed targets that can tempt us to teach to exams rather for the sheer joy of encouraging learning in students. This may tempt us to stop looking to experiment and pursue ever more interesting ways of teaching.

- Pupils who may still not seem to respond favourably towards us. (Try not to lose faith.)

Advice

There are many reasons why young people will misbehave. We need to recognize and understand these if we are to respond in a way that will be most effective.

 We should always refer back to our central purpose and mission. If we lose sight of this, then the road ahead can become obscure and rocky with lots of pitfalls. It is worth thinking about, for example, why students might be reluctant to engage with us in schools. People will argue that this could include any of the following:

- Violence seen on TV
- Computer games
- Racial tensions
- Gang cultures, guns, knives and violence on our streets
- Drugs and alcohol
- The influence of popular song lyrics
- Particular psychological problems
- Food additives
- The weather
- Phases of the moon (listen to Peter Gabriel and 'More than This' on the *Growing Up* album)
- A 'factory style' of educating children (Peter Senge and others have talked a lot about this)
- Inappropriate teaching styles
- Diet.

 You could no doubt instantly add further examples to this list (probably thousands). On top of these things there are the influences that come from the family.

Application

Making a difference and understanding behaviour motivators

With so many external pressures and worries that students may have, it is remarkable that more of them do not create problems in our schools/colleges. We therefore have a real challenge as most of what influences a student is beyond our control. But schools/colleges and teachers can and do make a difference. We can make a real difference to the life chances of the students we guide. Our school/college may be the only place where they sense any stability, order and security in their otherwise chaotic lives. Many studies show that a great deal of the success these students can have depends on them having a supportive relationship with at least one adult.

Rudolf Dreikurs identified four basic motivations for behaviour. He also said that these can generate counter-feelings in the adult. They can be summarized as follows:

Behaviour motivator of a student		Counter-feelings generated in you, the adult
A	Avoidance of failure	Feeling inadequate, helpless, fearful
B	Attention	Feeling annoyance
C	Anger/Revenge	Feeling anger and vengeful
D	Power	Feeling stubborn and wanting control

However logical we believe we are, and however much we therefore imagine that we can react to situations with a cool head, we are all driven by emotions that we find hard to prevent from taking over, particularly in difficult and challenging circumstances. These emotions can make us react to a situation in a way that is not always the most effective nor the way we would like to have reacted if we had had more time to reflect and analyse the situation. As a result, we can at times make the situation worse. All teachers will have experienced this at some time in their careers. You may have set out with a certain plan and before you know it you are deflected into a situation that benefits no one and tears the original plan apart. What we need to do is understand from the behaviour of a student the feelings we are experiencing and, as a result, the true motive of the student's behaviour. If we do this, we can then react in a way that allows us to make rational and logical decisions that then enable the lesson to continue to flow. This is so important, and so rarely considered that it is truly worth spending some time looking at each of the student motivators and our most likely 'natural' reaction in turn.

'Children require guidance and sympathy far more than instruction.'

Annie Sullivan

(A) Behaviour motivator – avoidance of failure

Sometimes we may get a strong reaction to something that to us seems to be a perfectly everyday, simple and non-threatening request.

Imagine this situation:
It is the start of a new year and your first lesson with a class. After an initial introduction to the lesson you ask the class to open their books, read page 22 and try to think about an answer to question 1.

Resultant student behaviour:
A student called Susan swears under her breath and walks to the door saying out loud 'I've had enough of this. I don't want to open my book and I'm not going to.'

What would your reaction be? For some teachers it could be this:
'Susan, I will not accept this kind of language and behaviour. Go and stand outside the principal's office.'

The subsequent (secondary) reaction-behaviour of the student may be:
Susan's behaviour escalates. She may swear again, this time directly at the teacher and run out of the school.

But what would this have achieved? By apparently dealing with the situation firmly and immediately we may feel we have shown who is boss. We have demonstrated to the rest of the class that this kind of behaviour is unacceptable. But at what cost? What is very unlikely is that Susan will say 'You know what Miss, I was acting stupidly and you have made me understand this now. Would you allow me to return to my seat?'

Advice

Question: What do you think the potential costs might be?

Answer: The teacher's relationship with Susan may have been significantly damaged and take a lot of time to repair. The teacher will also probably feel very dissatisfied with the way the whole scenario has unfolded.

So what I am going to suggest now is something that may be counter-intuitive.

An alternative reaction from the teacher could be:
The teacher walks over to the student's seat and calmly says 'Susan, I hear what you're saying. Come back to your seat and I'll open the book for you.'

And the alternative reaction-behaviour of the student:
The student walks back to her seat and sits down and begins to work with the teacher.

What do you feel about this? Some people may believe that this simply wouldn't work. My only response to this is that having seen many teachers operate in their classrooms over the past 25 years, I have witnessed these kinds of strategies working. Some people will also say that they think that Susan has won and the teacher has given in. They may feel that the teacher has been soft and weak in her approach. Again, in this case we need always to think about what we are trying to achieve. I would suggest that we want to enjoy teaching the class, we want them to learn, we want to have a positive atmosphere in the classroom, and we want to build relationships with all our students. Which of the strategies above will help us to achieve this most effectively?

Think: It is interesting to consider the possible reasons why Susan reacted the way she did to what seems on the face of it to be a perfectly reasonable request. These could be:

● Susan has had an argument last night with her mother.

● Susan has just fallen out with her best friend.

● Susan is embarrassed about her level of reading ability.

Application

Further thoughts about the behaviour motivator that is avoidance of failure

Clearly the actual reason for Susan's misbehaviour could be any one or more of the explanations listed on the previous page. Suppose that the true reason is that Susan is embarrassed about her level of reading ability. She won't want to tell the teacher this for the simple reason that she is embarrassed to admit this. If we are honest, none of us would want to feel stupid in front of other people. Susan is exactly the same. She is far happier to be punished for poor behaviour rather than to expose her weakness to the potential glare of the rest of her peers and the teacher. If Susan is told to leave the class, as will often be the case in such a situation, this will provide her with a way out of what for her is a terrible situation. On top of this there is a strange paradox. The teacher believes that he is punishing Susan for her poor behaviour, whereas Susan *wants* to leave the classroom because she doesn't want to read. She is being rewarded therefore for poor behaviour.

A number of people may still feel that the teacher has given in and 'lost'. Looking at a situation in terms of win or lose for the teacher or the student is not really what we are trying to do in a classroom. If we do want to look at it in a win or lose way, then I would argue that there is now a win–win situation that preserves the original intent of the lesson. Win–win is the only combination we should aim for. Here the teacher has enabled Susan to return to her seat and will then help her to get started with the task. The rest of the students will see the teacher as someone who really does want to help them if they have difficulties. They are given the message that poor behaviour will not allow them to escape the lesson. They also know that if they are having difficulty, the teacher will help them. The students will feel safe in this environment and this will enhance their chances to learn. Susan has preserved her dignity and is able to get on with her work and make progress. A sense of stability and purpose is restored that will also help with further lessons.

Question: Do you still feel that Susan's poor behaviour is left un-addressed?

Answer: Susan's behaviour must definitely be addressed. If this doesn't happen, it would be a disaster. The teacher in this case will pick up on the behaviour of Susan at a later stage. Susan must be guided into understanding how to behave appropriately in order to achieve what she wants. She must be aware that poor behaviour does have consequences. The reality is that the teacher will deal with the behaviour; it is only the time when it is dealt with that has changed.

Question: Is this approach harder than taking a more reactive 'you do as you are told' approach?

Answer: This approach does require more thought than taking immediate action in the classroom – but that immediate action could potentially have been explosive. It is not necessarily instinctive to react in the way described because the student's motivation for their behaviour (avoidance of failure) will stir powerful emotions or counter feelings in us that are a mixture of a fear of failure, a feeling of being inadequate because the situation has arisen and therefore a feeling of being somewhat helpless. Our flight or fight instincts kick in as soon as we are threatened. The trouble is that the flight or fight response can be stirred in us in situations where a more considered approach is required. This is why we have got to be aware of what we are doing in order that we don't act in haste and regret at our leisure.

'All who have meditated on the art of governing mankind have been convinced that the fate of empires depends on the education of youth.'

Aristotle

(B) Behaviour motivator – attention

Imagine this situation:
You are teaching a class. They are all involved in small group activities.

Resultant student behaviour:
In one group, Harry is no longer taking part in the activity but is instead humming in a way that the teacher can obviously hear him.

What would your reaction be? For some teachers it could be this:
The teacher asks Harry to stop humming but he simply continues. The teacher says to Harry that if he doesn't stop he will have to leave the room.

The subsequent (secondary) reaction-behaviour of the student may be:
Harry has a decision to make. He may stop but he may decide to dig his heels in. In this case he decides to dig his heels in. He continues to hum even louder and refuses to leave the room. The teacher therefore asks another student to get the head of year who comes to the lesson and after a short period of time manages to persuade Harry to leave the classroom.

Again we need to consider what has been achieved? It is true to say that Harry has now been removed from the class but at what cost in this situation? It is a fairly standard process to follow a behaviour management system that consists of a series of stages that include both warnings and consequences. The problem here is that the situation has simply got worse. We must always consider what we are trying to achieve. Here the teacher's goal was for all the pupils to engage in group activities. When Harry was unwilling to do this, the teacher's aim should have been to try to re-engage him with the activity so that he and the rest of the group could continue with their work.

Question: What do you think the potential costs might be? This time I will leave you to decide.

The alternative strategy that the teacher might adopt is again in some ways counter-intuitive and difficult for many people to accept.

An alternative reaction from the teacher could be:
The teacher asks Harry if he will help her set up the whiteboard for the activity that follows the group work.

And the alternative reaction-behaviour of the student:
Harry is deflected from his original disruptive behaviour and is happy to help the teacher and show his expertise in being able to assist her with the technical skills involved in preparing the follow-up activity. The teacher thanks Harry for his help. He returns to seat.

So what do you feel about this? Some people will believe that 'helping tasks' should be reserved for students who are behaving well. We need to challenge this belief if we are going to be able to use this behaviour management technique.

It is now interesting to consider the possible reasons why Harry reacted the way he did to what seems on the face of it to be a perfectly reasonable request. These could be:

- Harry doesn't like working in the group and therefore was drawing attention to this fact by trying to seek attention.
- Harry felt inadequate in the group activity and therefore was looking for a way out by drawing attention to himself and therefore involving the teacher in taking action.
- Harry was bored and simply seeking attention.

Application

Further thoughts about the behaviour motivator that is attention seeking

In the situation described on the previous page, the teacher will probably feel angry about the student's behaviour. This is a good indicator that the behaviour motivator has to do with attention-seeking. As the student is seeking attention, we all have the choice of providing this attention in one of two ways. One way is to draw attention to the behaviour and use the warning and consequences strategy to try to get it to stop. If you think that this is going to work, then it is perfectly valid to use this. There is never just one method that should be used to solve all circumstances. This is why behaviour management can appear at times to be so complex. In the situation described, this was in fact the first strategy used but it clearly doesn't work and therefore the desired aim of the lesson is being impacted upon. An alternative strategy is to engage the student in another activity that deflects them from their original feelings of discontent and allows them to be involved in a constructive task that benefits the class.

As with any technique, it is important to consider the potential pitfalls. Here it would be unwise to give the implicit message that being disruptive results in a reward. This would then reinforce poor behaviour. It is therefore essential not to simply employ this technique in a reactionary way. Rather, we need to be proactive and consider the very best ways of using the deflection or alternative task strategy. Using the description we looked at earlier, we need to be 'consciously competent' in what we are doing. As we build up a range of these strategies, we may eventually operate them in an unconsciously competent way a lot of the time. We have grown to know (subconsciously) that they work. They have become a habit that we instinctively use. This does not mean though that we shouldn't continually try to find new ways of employing proactive deflection strategies.

Advice

What deflection methods do you presently employ in your classroom? If you don't employ deflection methods, can you think of any that you might try out?

Remember

It is essential not to simply employ the deflection or alternative task strategy technique in a reactionary way. Rather, we need to be proactive and consider the very best ways of using it.

'Creativity is a type of learning process where the teacher and pupil are located in the same individual.'

Arthur Koestler

Application

(C) Behaviour motivator – anger/revenge

Imagine this situation:
You are teaching a class. One of your class rules is that students should not be chewing gum in the lessons.

Resultant student behaviour:
Fiona is 14 years old. She is laughing and disrupting students around her and chewing gum.

What would your reaction be? For some teachers it could be this:
You ask Fiona to take the chewing gum out of her mouth and put it in the bin near the door.

The subsequent (secondary) reaction-behaviour of the student may be:
Fiona gets up out of her seat walks over to the bin and appears to be doing what she is asked to do. However, she then kicks the bin over, opens the door, swears at the teacher and slams the door.

Oh dear! Fiona is clearly angry and her anger may naturally stir anger in us as well. We may therefore decide to storm after Fiona and insist that she should 'come back to the room this minute'. We may be very lucky and Fiona may return to the classroom, but on the whole this course of action will most probably cause Fiona to escalate her own inappropriate behaviour even more. In addition, are we really lucky if Fiona returns to the classroom? Do we really want her back in when she is so angry? And if we do take this course, the potential costs may be significant in a variety of other ways.

Advice

Question: What do you think the potential costs might be? Again I will leave you to decide.

So what is the alternative strategy that we might employ here?

An alternative reaction from the teacher could be:
You allow Fiona to leave the classroom without running after her. You re-engage with the class immediately and direct your attention to the lesson and their learning.

And the alternative reaction-behaviour of the student:
Fiona walks away from the classroom and has to now make further decisions about her next course of action. She has created this situation and must now reflect on the consequences of her behaviour so far and her next step.

How do you feel about this course of action? It is hard for us to let go of certain situations but this is what is being suggested here.

It is now interesting to consider the possible reasons why Fiona reacted the way she did. What might these be?

Application

Further thoughts about the behaviour motivator that is anger or revenge

Planned ignoring, which is what this strategy is about, can seem to run against what some people feel to be the most effective ways of managing a class. Like so many of these strategies, I can perfectly well understand this feeling and I have had to struggle myself to understand that these strategies work. Why? Well because it just doesn't necessarily come naturally to us. But then again what seems to be natural and 'common sense' does not necessarily give us the most effective ways of dealing with what are complex human behaviours. In addition, it is important to model to students what we expect of them. We should demonstrate to them that 'planned ignoring' is useful in situations where they themselves may be being provoked. This could happen to them in a playground, for example. In this situation our advice may often be that the best action is to ignore the deliberate provocation. If, therefore, in our example here we as the teacher run after Fiona, we are modelling to them that we are not prepared to use planned ignoring ourselves to resolve a situation effectively. If we do use planned ignoring, we would need to instruct all our students very clearly, both implicitly and possibly explicitly, that planned ignoring is what we are doing as part of our normal behaviour. At the same time they will need to know from us that we will pick up on Fiona's behaviour at a later point when we can deal with it in a rational way that does not affect the learning of the class.

Advice

In what circumstances would you use planned ignoring tactics in your classroom? What strategies would you use to ensure that the behaviour is addressed at a later time?

Remember

Planned ignoring may go against the grain but we have to be clear about how we can deal with a situation most effectively. Creating a storm is not going to help us or the student or our future relationship.

'Prejudices, it is well known, are most difficult to eradicate from the heart whose soil has never been loosened or fertilized by education; they grow there, firm as weeds among rocks.'

Charlotte Brontë

(D) Behaviour motivator – power/control

Imagine this situation:
You are teaching a class and notice a boy called David wearing a leather jacket. This is not part of the school uniform and coats are not allowed to be worn in lessons in any case. You remind David of the school rule.

Resultant student behaviour:
David just ignores your instruction.

What would your reaction be? For some teachers it could be this:
To walk over to David and insist that he takes off his jacket.

The subsequent (secondary) reaction-behaviour of the student may be:
David still refuses to take off his jacket. He says he is cold.

A power struggle has now developed. David is wanting to exert his authority and so do you. Who will win? Again we are in a win–lose situation that we don't want to be part of – particularly in front of a watchful class.

Advice

Question: What do you think the potential costs might be? Again I will leave you to decide.

As before, we need to remind ourselves about what we are trying to do in the class. What we want is for students to further their learning in a positive atmosphere that is conducive to that learning taking place. Will a theatrical power-struggle assist this?

An alternative reaction from the teacher could be:
You simply carry on with the lesson after having asked David to remove his jacket and he has refused to do so.

And the alternative reaction-behaviour of the student:
David now has a choice to make. He has already disobeyed a simple instruction that you will deal with later on. He can continue with the lesson with his jacket on, remove his jacket or escalate the misbehaviour.

The action we are taking here can again be described as 'planned ignoring'. This is not taking no action. Instead it is a very deliberate part of our behaviour-management techniques. Do we want a student who is refusing to abide by a school rule to sabotage our planned lesson? The answer must be no.

It is now interesting to consider the possible reasons why David reacted the way she did. What might these be?

Further thoughts about the behaviour motivator that is power or control

At some stage later on, we must be prepared to address David's misbehaviour. We may ask him to stay behind after the lesson and talk to him then. What can be surprising is that what David tells us makes us completely change our view of this minor infringement of a school rule.

A summary of what we want to achieve, and motivations for behaviour

In our journey to becoming effective behaviour managers we must always expect the unexpected. We can then be in a position to proactively deal with any situations that arise. The worst course of action is to blindly step into situations without thinking and without being prepared. If we do this, we can find ourselves reacting in a way that simply escalates any initial misbehaviour into something far bigger. What we have looked at in this chapter are a series of ways to view any difficult behaviour we might encounter. The steps in this process involve the following:

Step 1	Always think, 'What was my original goal?' Any action should not deviate you from this when dealing with everyday behaviour issues.

Step 2	Then think about what the student's true motivation for their behaviour might be. Don't allow yourself at this stage to be ruled by natural instincts that are reactions to their behaviour. Ensure flight or fight instincts don't kick in.

Step 3	Next think about whether conventional behaviour-management techniques involving warnings and consequences are likely to achieve the outcome you desire. Could they actually make the situation worse?

Step 4	Now think what kind of strategies you might employ to achieve your aim. We have discussed here how offering help, involving the student in a diversionary task, and using the planned ignoring technique can all be helpful.

Step 5	Finally, we must think about how we follow up any inappropriate behaviour. The aim of this should be to assist the student in recognizing appropriate ways of behaving that they can use now in the school/college environment and indeed through the rest of their lives. It may be that they need guidance in terms of developing skills that allow them to express themselves in an assertive but non-aggressive way.

Advice

Finally

I hope that this book will enable you to become the kind of educator you always wanted to be. We are all educators in whatever walk of life we may be involved in. People learn from our actions. We can guide them both implicitly and explicitly. In schools and colleges the accumulation of new knowledge and the growth of the education of all members is intense. We have a tremendous opportunity to make this as effective as possible by thorough and comprehensive coaching that involves everyone. A major area of that coaching is in the field of effective behaviour management. If this book has helped you in your journey to be in a position of excellence in terms of all your skills and characteristics as an educator and effective behaviour coach, then the job of this book is done. This is what we must strive to achieve – we must never cease to have the dream. We may even now be on the threshold of that dream.

Further reading and other sources of information

Hay McBer (2000) *A Model of Teacher Effectiveness* (Hay McBer Report). London: DfEE

Swainston, T. (2002) *Effective Teachers* (Vital 1), Stafford: Network Educational Press

Swainston, T. (2003) *Effective Teachers in Primary Schools*, Stafford: Network Educational Press

wik.ed.uiuc.edu/index.php/Dreikurs_Rudolf

Answers to Bullying Questionnaire, page 63

The shocking reality is that all of these statements are true.